M000206346

Barbara Knudson, Ph.D.

Living in Chaos, Walking in Peace

A Matter of Ascension

[signature: Barbara Knudson]

Legendary Publishing

Boise, Idaho

© 1998 by Barbara Knudson, Ph.D.

Living in Chaos, Walking in Peace: A Matter of Ascension

All rights reserved. No part of this book may be used, reproduced or transmitted in any form by any means, electronic or mechanical, including photocopying and recording, or by any information storage or retrieval system, in any manner except in the case of brief quotations embodied in critical articles and reviews. Requests for such permission should be submitted in writing to the publisher.

The author of this book does not, directly or indirectly, dispense medical advice nor prescribe the use of any technique contained herein as a form of treatment for physical or mental problems. For specific physical or mental issues, please seek out the assistance of a medical or psychological expert. The intent of the author is to offer options that may be useful in the quest for spiritual and personal transformation.

Library of Congress Number: 98-67109

Spiritual/New Age

International Standard Book Number (ISBN): 1-887747-20-6

Printed in the United States

Illustrations and Cover Design: Richard Terra/Terra Nova

Cover Picture: Anna Smith

First U.S. Edition

This book is published by:

Legendary Publishing Company
P.O. Box 7706
Boise, Idaho 83707-1706
U.S.A.

Dedicated to Jim Fields, my husband,
my partner, my best friend,
my love, and my mirror.

PREFACE

As I work on this book, I see three blind men and an elephant. I know that I am one of the blind men trying to make sense of something too large for me to comprehend. This book is my view of the elephant. I want to honor your view of the elephant so that together we may get a greater sense of the whole.

It seems as if my life has been on fast forward. For the past five years Jim, my husband, and I have spent almost every weekend driving 250 miles from Boise to our other home near Twin Falls, Idaho, where my father, who has Parkinson's and Alzheimer's, lived with a full-time caretaker. Life was so hectic that we had little or no time to ourselves as a couple. One day on the drive back to Boise we were talking about what we would do someday when "things get back to normal." Suddenly we looked at each other and started laughing. This *was* normal!

Another time while I was driving back to Boise by myself after a particularly challenging weekend of laying out medications, buying groceries, mowing lawn — and stressed to the max — I asked God if I couldn't go on cruise control for a little while. I needed just a little rest from the chaos. The answer I got was an emphatic, *NO!*

For years I had spent some of my time and energy on my own emotional healing, but now I realized every minute of every day could become my healing journey. I seemed to be living in perpetual chaos. This healing process was to be my life journey and if I wanted to have peace, I had better pay attention to the lessons being offered. All these experiences were opportunities for learning, for finishing unfinished business, and for experiencing joy.

As I looked more closely, I noticed fear was often the bottom line culprit of my discomfort — fear of death, fear of success, fear of rejection, fear of unknowns, fear of not enough time, fear, fear, and more fear. Like a scared little rabbit, I seemed to be jumping at every little noise, frightened to totally participate in life. I had been working on this book for over ten years! Ah yes, fear.

Oh, there were lots of other emotions too. Stuffed inside me , they sometimes leaked out on my family and friends in the form of criticism and irritation. Even with all my self therapy, I still was not at the place of peace I knew was possible even in the middle of chaos. Now seemed the time, for if not now, when? And then, Ascension ideas started entering my awareness. I had a focus. Here was a path to peace.

There are many parts of the elephant I have yet to explore. You may have seen the elephant from a different perspective and perhaps you can share your views with me. This book is my journey. The first part of the book, *Ascension: Heaven on Earth*, explores some of the different ways of looking at the changes we are experiencing here on Earth. The second part of the book, *The Healing Journey*, offers some practical tips for personal healing and some pragmatic exercises for finding more peace in your life. The third part of the book, *Being a Light Worker*, stretches you into the spiritual realm for the healing of yourself and of others.

I am most grateful to my father who continually encouraged my exploration of the far side of the elephant. He taught me how to dowse, he gave me my first self-hypnosis book which allowed me to mind travel to the far reaches of the Universe, and he located the Silva Mind Method for me.

I am also grateful to my mother, my husband and my daughter. How wise of me to place myself in this family! It is those closest to us who most easily mirror our unfinished business. My family is willing to love me enough to be in my face, to be my angel blessings. How brave they are to travel this road with me.

Did you know that the 'world is flat' is still a common perception? It must be, for many times I would start to talk about my journeys to discover the other elephant parts, and people would look me in the eye and say: *You don't believe that!* So, it is with extreme gratitude that I honor my parents, husband, daughter, sister and close friends who listened to my perceptions, encouraged my stories, and supported me in the writing of this book.

To all the people who love me, the journey in this book is theirs too.

Barbara Knudson

1998

LIVING IN CHAOS, WALKING IN PEACE
A MATTER OF ASCENSION

PART I: ASCENSION: HEAVEN ON EARTH   1

    This Thing Called Death   7

    Multiple Realities   13

    Ascension and the Veil   19

PART II: THE HEALING JOURNEY   25

    Life as Illusion   31

    Creating Realities with Living Affirmations   37

    Mirror, Mirror on the Wall   47

PART III: BEING A LIGHT WORKER   57

    Energetic Clearings   65

    Creating Personal Sacred Space   81

    Healing Places   85

    Putting It All Together   89

BIBLIOGRAPHY   95

ILLUSTRATIONS

Figure 1   page 39

Figure 2   page 72

Figure 3   page 73

Figure 4   page 74

Figure 5   page 75

Figure 6   page 76

Figure 7   page 77

ASCENSION: HEAVEN ON EARTH

Divine Creator, who art everywhere, hallowed be thy name.
Thy Kingdom come, thy will be done
on Earth as it is in Heaven.

As we approach the millenium, the media is filled with doomsday predictions. Weather patterns seem to be more erratic. Inversions settle over my little city of Boise, Idaho. The nightly news is filled with reports of volcanoes, floods, tornadoes, and earthquakes around the world. Terrorism comes to the United States. People I see in my practice seem overwhelmed, overworked, and unable to find time for the self. My time and energy used to be focused on a community. Now I focus on the world. It is as if the rest of the world is running my life and with some dire predictions for the future!

Is there a quickening of events, including Earth changes? Do the prophecies speak to us about this time? Are we in the "Shift of the Ages" as prophesied by the ancients? Will the year 2000 be the end of time as we know it, as the planets align across the sky? Why does the Mayan calendar end in 2012? What do the Hindu, Mayan, Hopi, and Aztec predict for this time? Why are there species of birds showing up where not seen before and whales beaching themselves? Is the weather worsening? Will Earth changes create economic crisis? Should I spend all my savings for there may be no old age to worry about? Should I meditate on energy enhancement and disappear into a high vibration, as noted in the best selling book, *The Celestine Prophecy*? Should I store food and be prepared to head for the hills? Is the photon belt fast approaching to zap us right out of our bodies?

Time seems to be contracting and space seems to be expanding. Television shows reflect hope and hopelessness. We see more shows on prophecies and the end of Earth as we know it, but there are also more shows on angels and hope. Is this Armageddon? Or, are we ascending? I experience confusion and fear. What should I do?

Earth is changing; we are changing. Gregg Braden, in *Walking Between the Worlds: the Science of Compassion*, suggested planetary frequencies are increasing and planetary magnetics are decreasing. This "shift of the ages" is a measurable, evolutionary event now underway. The electromagnetic change in the Earth impacts each of us. According to Braden, the human species is also changing at a cellular level. Our earthly biological self is electromagnetic; the range of magnetism and frequency governs our body.

Braden noted that if we could be viewed as electromagnetic individuals, we would each uniquely appear as a composite wave of geometric patterns. Looking from the view of Unified Field Theory, we find that we are one, that a change in one aspect, in the Earth or in ourselves, affects change in all aspects. Eric

Klein, in the introduction of *The Crystal Stair: A Guide to Ascension*, suggested that each of us will shift into the next dimension of consciousness as the Earth shifts. Braden suggested that the end result of these electro-magnetic changes is Ascension.

Brooke Medicine Eagle, in her audiotape *Awakening in the Golden Age*, said that according to the Aztec calendar, we are at the bottom of the 13th hell, the most dense and violent of times. Using information from her teacher, Rob Cox, Brooke shared the concept of the photon belt, a band of light covered by a sheath, through which the Earth passes approximately every 15,000 years as our solar system moves through the twelve astrological houses of the heavens. As we enter the sheath, it is as dark as possible. When we move into the intense band of light, this huge voltage will zap everything electromagnetic. Imagine plugging yourself into a 1,000 volt electrical socket and you get a small idea of the impact of the Light.

Once into the belt, the age of enlightment, or being in the Light, lasts about 1,000 years. Ancient prophets have suggested it will be a glorious time. As generations pass and the Earth begins to move away from the band, people will begin to forget the ease and aspects of the Light. Six to ten thousand years ago Seers noticed they were beginning to forget the previous experiences of being in the Light, so they recorded their stories. These stories are now being studied.

For this prophesied shift of the ages, Brooke Medicine Eagle suggests an event; Gregg Braden suggests an evolution. Both may be true; neither may be true. But we do know that how we structured our world yesterday is being challenged from both the world of science and the world of spirit. This "shift of the ages" is a shift that melds science and spirit.

So, does this mean the end of the world as we know it? Probably! There is no doubt that the world is changing. We are in a tremendous paradigm shift. Just recently a huge source of energy was discovered, a star a million times larger than our sun, whose energy is only beginning to reach us. However, the Earth has always been in flux; great stars have always been there. With global communications we are just more aware of the changes in the climate, in the Earth's surface, in the economic issues, in diseases and in famine as they affect those in all parts of our globe. With technology, we are also beginning to map the impact of changes in the Universe. The results of these continual changes are unknown and it is the unknown that is most fearful for us. We like control — control of ourselves, of others, and of the Earth.

In my meditations, in the non-material reality, I am warned that NOW is the time to learn to live without fear. The shift of the ages is now!

So how can I be peaceful in this paradigm shift? What is my role in these chaotic times?

In July 1997 I attended the **Universal Light Workers Conference** in Seattle. There were over 400 registered participants! Themes at the conference included sacred geometry; time collapsing; space expanding; multiple realities; Hopi prophecy; new paradigms for leadership; God consciousness; and ascension. The emphasis was on hope and intention. So what in my life took me to such a conference?

In 1992 I attended a Spirituality conference in Boise where I won a Tarot reading. I had never had a Tarot reading so that seemed rather intriguing to me. During the session, I mentioned to the reader that I had this sense of loneliness inside me that I referred to as

4

existential loneliness; that is, the loneliness of everyone. I also told her that I always teased my family that I came from Alpha Centauri. At some level, I felt I had been mistakenly birthed into this body on Earth. It did not feel like home to me.

The Tarot reader suggested I meditate to see if I could get some answers about my origins and the loneliness I felt. It seemed like a good suggestion to me.

At home, I quieted myself with a few deep breaths, stated my intention and found myself flying through the Universe at light speed. I noticed what seemed to be a city, but nothing like what I had ever experienced, even in my wildest imagination! Unseen Beings seemed to move from place to place by being carried on a movement of air, rather than by walking. In this manner, I was escorted to a specific place in this city. I entered a room and said, *Oh, you have bedrooms just like ours.* Their response was, *We have created this for your comfort.* The voice continued, *Would you like to meet your original mother and father?* I turned to see two wonderful Beings of Light, separate, but almost merging with each other.

I felt their profound love. I began to cry as I experienced this love beyond words. We communicated for a while, as I continued to cry. Then I was asked if I would like to see myself. Surprised, I said, *Yes!* They directed me to turn and look into the mirror. I turned and saw myself reflected. I, too, was a Light Being! I was beautiful and full of the same love I had experienced with my original Mother and Father. It was wonderful!

I was then told that I had chosen to fulfill an Earth experience at this time and that I needed to return and complete that agreement. It would have been easy to stay in this place where I felt such profound love, but I knew it was important to honor my agreement. I was told that I could visit at any time, if I ever felt lonely or disconnected again.

I returned to my earthly realm. I have never again felt lonely and disconnected. I still feel that wonderful flame of love inside. Just remembering the experience brings tears of joy. I am so very grateful for the experience. Even if it was just a figment of my imagination, I am changed forever and I know who and what I am. In my very essence, I am a Light Being come to Earth with purpose.

I just wasn't sure about my purpose or my agreement. Why was I here?

THIS THING CALLED DEATH

For a long time, based on my early religious upbringing, I imagined that once I died I put on a long white robe, got some wings and floated around a lot. Then about ten years or so ago, I started having very traumatic death dreams — earth upheavals, plane crashes, being shot. I just died a lot and woke up very unrested and tired. Even in my meditations, I died!

One night I dreamed I was in an office. Someone asked me to make coffee. I told them I didn't make coffee. Pretty normal behavior for me. I then left work and walked out into the parking lot. In my lucid self in the dream I was quite pleased that this was not a death dream. But instead of getting into a car, I just lifted off the ground. Cool! I like flying dreams. I flew over a grove of trees, saw some tiny little horses, talked with their owner and then headed off to a school yard where I was to pick up a teenage boy. Two needed to be picked up, but I was responsible for one. He had not learned to fly so we struggled along in the air as I taught him how to imagine lightness and floating.

We reached a big rock wall and, with great effort on both our parts, got over it to the other side. We visited with some folks on this other side, but most of them were sitting in rockers facing television screens mounted on the south wall. Each television screen was encircled with a big, beautiful floral wreath. Very lovely.

As I looked at the television screens I saw coffins. Great! This *was* another death dream! All the people were watching their own funerals! About that time, I heard beautiful music. A magnificent white light shone through the west window. Everyone got up from their rockers and moved into the Light. I was not invited. I asked, *Hey, am I dead or alive?* A voice answered, *Barbara, it doesn't matter for you will be doing the same work dead or alive — forever!*

Well, that about blew me over. You mean I had to work after I died?

Affirmative and infinitely, came the response. So was this to be my work?

Yes, came the response. *I am to help people over the wall?* I asked. *Yes, and more,* came the response.

As I have meditated on this dream, I have come to see that my life purpose is to be a facilitator of transitions — for the living, for those dying and for those already dead. Was there no difference between Heaven and Earth? Talk about a paradigm shift!

According to the polls, a great number of people believe in life after death. Books on near death experiences can be found in any bookstore. Although the reported stories, as well as religious orientations, have many similarities, there are also many dissimilarities. So in Heaven does one person go to the Nevada Heaven and another to New York City Heaven? Well, yes, sort of, depending on your source of information.

During the period from 1992 to 1997, I scaled back much of my community work to spend time with family. It was chaotic. It was about death and dying. In the 1980s my father was diagnosed with Parkinson's Disease. It is a progressively, debilitating disease. My father, my friend, my teacher, my encourager, my hero, was disintegrating before my eyes. This once strong, gentle man now had bouts of depression and anger. His mind was also fading and he knew it. As the years ravaged his body, the disease spread with Alzheimer's symptoms to his mind. My mother could no longer deal with him. The family moved him into our home. He was dying, but dying slowly. One does not die of Parkinson's. It ravages the body and kills the mind, but the body lives on and on. I wanted to help.

It was time to learn about dying. My friend, Peggy, recommended *Deathing*, which led to the *Tibetan Book of Living and Dying*. According to this book and to the beliefs of many indigenous people, in the death bardo, that time directly after spirit lift-off from the body, one goes to the place he or she is thinking about. Hell is hell, Heaven is Heaven, and fishing is fishing. Thought becomes reality. If one is thinking of Jesus, one might see Jesus, or Buddha, or angels, or heavenly hosts, or hell. If on our death bed we are thinking of all the mean things people have done to us, we may find ourselves in a place where people do mean things to us. There seems to be the reality of this life and then there is what we know as death of a body. There also seems to be a reality, after death, where we live without the benefit of this particular dense body; but we live in this other reality with non-material bodies very recognizable to others occupying this space that we call Heaven.

Monroe, in his book *Journeys Out of the Body*, called the area nearest the physical world Locale II. Here reality is a result of our desires and of our fears. He suggested we be very aware of our thoughts, for in Locale II what we think is what we get. It appears that even in Heaven (or that part of Heaven with energy closest to Earth's) we create complete realities with the same belief systems with which we created on Earth.

In all mystical and most religious practices, there are prayers for the dead to remind the soul to go to the Light. The Light is there for all of us and we are welcomed into it with open arms, but not everyone seems to focus on the Light. We can get stuck in the death bardo of our own making. We get the whole kit and kaboodle of our mind creation. If our focus on earth was money or material good, or addictions, or sex, well guess what! As we pass through the stream of our memories, we may get stuck in one of these scenarios. According to Eric Klein, there are numerous heavens and hells, each with their own experience in this new fourth dimension. This may help explain the differences in near death experiences where some experience heavenly visions and others hellish nightmares. The prayers the living say for the dead are to remind the dead to go to the Light, but many of the dead seem to be as stubborn in the hereafter as when they were on Earth.

I was familiar with prayers for the dead and dying, but I was just beginning to discover that my flying teenager dream was a "search and rescue" dream, one of others I was to have, for people who died but were not able to make the transition into the Light. Some stay attached to Earth, not understanding they are no longer in body. Some create bardos of choice, although they do not seem to be aware they have a choice.

I have learned that search and rescue dreams or meditations are not that unusual. It is the task of shamans, priests, and monks (and regular people like me, who in their curiosity go to other realities to assist as guides) to rescue souls from their creations.

Monroe traveled with his mind to non-material spaces or bardos. He discovered that he was going on rescue missions to places where people were stuck in their death bardos, repeating their stories over and over, never knowing that the experiences were their creations. Just as the shaman or priest pleads with the soul to come with him, so did Monroe plead with the souls to come to the park where they would be met by loved ones who would assist them on their spiritual path.

In this fourth dimension it appears that the Bardo creation is very earth-like because, according to the stories, it can be difficult, and sometimes impossible, to convince a soul person that they can choose their reality to be different. And to think I thought my Earthly life was the only reality!

Multiple Realities

Carl Jung wondered if he was a man dreaming he was a butterfly or a butterfly dreaming he was a man. We dream dreams that are so real we wake up screaming. We cry at movies. We enter virtual realities through technology. We travel to the underworld, middle world, or upper world on soul journeys. In our minds, we plan our future during dull business meetings. Much of our life is spent thinking about the past or about the future. Much of our life is spent in imagining.

Imagination is a fairly recent word in man's vocabulary. We often use it to discount another's reality. *Oh, that's just your imagination!* But for many indigenous people, the experience, dream, vision, or shape-shifting is the reality of the now, with little, if any, emphasis on the past or the future.

Our physical self does not distinguish between our thoughts about external events and actual external events. Think about a lemon. Imagine rolling it across the counter, softening it under the pressure of your hand. Lift it to your nose. Smell it. Take a knife and slice it. Squeeze the lemon juice onto your tongue. Notice how your mouth puckers up even as you think about the taste of the lemon juice in your mouth. And yet there is no lemon juice actually in your mouth, just in your imagination! Our bodies respond to our thoughts as real. In the dentist's chair, I travel to safe and sacred places in my mind and thus avoid those dreadful, mouth numbing shots! I use imagination.

While living in Denver in the 1970s, I attended a Silva Mind Method seminar. The seminars are designed to assist participants in developing their own psychic and healing abilities. In one of the exercises we developed a laboratory in our mind. We created files, computers, viewing screens, male and female guides, healing potions, whatever we thought might be useful. We decorated our mind laboratories to fit our personalities. It was here that we could go to gather information and to work. We even created a bulletin board where other people, using the same technique, could leave us a note, much like the electronic mail functions on our computers today. It was a fun exercise!

We learned that all information of the universe is available to everyone. It is just a matter of accessing the information. To be psychic, you just access information already available in the universe. To be an Einstein, you just access information. To write a great novel, you just access information. To be an Edgar Cayce, you just access information. Of course, accessing information does not mean you will automatically understand it. Knowing about math and physics helps to understand some of the laws of the universe!

Near the end of the seminar, we were given a card with a name, gender, and age of someone not in the room but known to someone in the room. We were each to do a reading and a healing on that person. I had written down Karrie, my daughter, and handed the card to the group leader.

The man who then got my daughter's card entered the Alpha state to do the reading. We were all novices and more than a little nervous. He sat with eyes closed for such a long time and *then* just started rapidly rattling off information. It was filled with details that I wrote down as quickly as possible. I am not very good at remembering such details and I wanted to be able to validate this information.

The man listed my daughter's accidents, and there were many, as well as the dates of the accidents. He described Karrie in detail. I was impressed! It had taken him a long time to get any information on her. I asked how he had finally gathered the information. He said he was not seeing any information, so he had "gone" to the laboratory he had created in his mind, opened his file cabinet, pulled out the file with Karrie's name, opened it, and just started reading the information.

What I had previously called vivid imagination now took on a new meaning. This was verifiable information from an imagined source. There were occasions when I had a "hit" on something floating across my mind, but I had never intentionally "gone" to a place in my mind for specific information. Imagination now became a much more useful tool.

I started paying more attention to my dreams, learning to be lucid in my dreams so that I could gather information and complete unfinished business. My meditation trips to faraway places in the Universe took on different meanings. It became more difficult for me to distinguish the validity of my "imagination" experience from my "real" experience. I started learning more about shape shifters and soul retrievals. I was in the kindergarten of the university of multiple realities. It was fascinating and so much fun!

If you have ever listened to two or more people describe the same experience, you certainly know that there are multiple realities existing simultaneously! I am sometimes certain my husband Jim must have another wife who shared the experiences he describes since my experiences of the same event are *so* much different. Even in experiencing the same moment together, we have different realities.

Sometimes, one of us "remembers" conversations in which the other apparently did not participate. You know the kind: *Yes, I did tell you that Mary's son is getting married next week.* Well, one of us must have been in another dimension for the message that was sent was not received.

Must have been in another dimension is now a standard joke at our house.

Some of the greatest travelers to other dimensions are the science fiction writers. *Star Trek, The Next Generation, Deep Space Nine,* and *Contact* are some well-known products of their imaginations. The television show *Sliders* seems to represent some of the current literature on multiple realities. Only now we will not need mechanical devices, only the thoughts in our minds, as we move from one reality to another. I swim with the dolphins at sea, walk in the Garden with Christ, and visit my original mother and father. All these experiences bring deep emotion. They seem real to me. Are there even more realities we have not even dreamed? For some the trees talk, while others bilocate. The new frontier is really one of multiple realities. Will they be the same for you and me, or will our thoughts create separate, simultaneous experiences?

Einstein, among others, planted the seeds of a new paradigm, called quantum physics. They realized that their current view of the physical world was incomplete. The old space-time model was replaced by a timeless, flowing field. Einstein and his colleagues proposed a new geometry that had no beginning or end, no edges, no solidity. Every solid particle in the Universe turned out to be vibrating energy. Based on our five senses, our third dimensional experience only *appears* to happen in a sequential order. The experiences of Monroe support this wave-vibration concept with different worlds all existing at different frequencies — with our earthly experience existing within one of those frequencies.

This quantum field is not separate from us, it *is* us. Although things outside ourselves appear to be real, there is no proof of reality apart from the observer. No two people experience exactly the same universe. According to quantum physics every world view creates its own world. We live simultaneously in multiple realities, maybe in more ways than we have yet to imagine.

Ascension and the Veil

So how does this mesh with Ascension? Well, for me Ascension means having the experience of Heaven that I would normally get only through death. That is, the veil of death becomes an illusion; I do not have to pass over to anywhere. I am in Heaven, in the Light, but this time I get to take a physical body.

Now imagine that we, in our prayers, meditations and loving compassionate thoughts, are creating a higher vibration for ourselves. Then let us suppose that changes in the external Universe, that is, planet alignment, photon belt, angelic intercession, are also quickening the vibration on this side of the veil equal to the vibration one has without a body. Imagine that in body we have learned ways to physically handle this increased vibration. There would then be no veil! Thought would be instant creation and we would be in body. There would be no death of the body. There would be just increased vibration, with less density, to a point of instant creation. Everyone would instantly create their own reality.

According to Klein, ascension is the goal of this Earthly third dimension. As you increase your frequency of vibration you move into realms once invisible to you. Ascension is the leap into another dimension, into a higher state of consciousness. Ascension is personal enlightment and transformation generated by our increased energetic vibration, present moment awareness and self healing.

At the Seattle conference, one of the speakers asked us if we were noticing that we were receiving quicker responses to our personal requests to the Universe, to our programming, to our affirmations. The general consensus was that we were. I thought that I was just getting better at paying attention to my thoughts and more specific in affirming my intentions. But the speaker suggested we were not just improving our abilities to create, but that the quickening, that increased vibration both of the Earth and of us, was making the veil less solid and we were more rapidly co-creating our worlds. This means that our thoughts have become even more powerful than before and are more quickly realized. Braden suggested that the Earth's lower magnetic fields provide the basis for quicker manifestation of thought. Earth's magnetic fields are changing and one of the things in Heaven, that is, manifestation of thought, is now more quickly happening on Earth.

As I reviewed some of the ascension literature, I noticed some differences between Heaven and Earth. In Heaven there is high vibration; low density body, present moment focus; and thought creates instantly. On Earth there is low vibration; high density body, past and future focus and thought usually takes time to create. But as I observe life and the world around me, I notice that these differences between Heaven and Earth have begun to decrease. And we, as Earthlings, can also intentionally decrease this difference.

Also I have noticed an increase in the number of miracles. These miracles may use the form of tools, such as new technology, new medicines, aroma therapy, Reiki, healing touch, or some of the newer counseling techniques, such as Eye Movement Desensitization and Reprocessing (EMDR), and Thought Field Therapy. But the results are often, more often than I have ever noticed before, instantaneous. In my own experience, physical pains of 30 years duration, that I thought permanent or in need of surgery, are now gone!

The miracles also happen on the psychological level. One night I woke up thinking about my mother. We had a real control struggle between us. Mostly when I thought of her I remembered all the things that she did that hurt or upset me and I got angry and frustrated. I knew that Mom had done many nice things for me, but they were never front and center in my memory. Rather, always present was the frustration, the anger.

As I lay in bed I said to the heavens *I want to understand this. I want to feel the loving memories of my mother. I want to love her totally.* And I, in the darkness did the EMDR therapeutic technique.

All of a sudden, I felt a rush through my body. I sobbed with love and compassion for my mother. All of the bad memories were gone. I could not even remember one. I was filled with loving memories of all Mom had done for me and I could only think of her with love and compassion. It has been so to this day.

I am most grateful for this experience. When Mom died suddenly, I felt nothing but total, unconditional love for her. I am so grateful for that instant healing in the middle of the night, that wonderful miracle.

Some of the other changes I have begun to notice are:

Things just don't bother me as much as
they used to;

I feel more at peace even when the world is
falling down around me;

I look for the cosmic humor even in chaotic
situations;

I am much more flexible in my interactions;

I become aware of my emotions and experiences more quickly and adjust them
according to my skills;

I have more interesting experiences that feel
multidimensional or transdimensional;

I wonder more often if I dreamed something or if it really happened;

I am more intuitive;

Synchronicity prevails in my life;

It is easier for me to understand how I am
ONE with the ALL and how each of us,
with totally different views of the elephant, is lovingly a part of the ALL, each
in our own unique way.

I believe this is a joyous time to be on Earth. True there may be dramatic, chaotic times, for that has been Earth's history. But as we increase our vibration, and bring more Light into our body, we will notice how thought more quickly becomes reality. We will experience more love, more compassion, for it is love and compassion that raises our vibration level.

Not everyone will focus on a path of Light, of Heaven on Earth. There are many paths, but I believe we all are ascending, for the Earth in its own way is also ascending.

We each have within us a Light, a seed, a vision of Heaven on Earth. But we try to make the vision fit within the reality we have created on Earth. What if we created new realities? What if we transformed our fears? What if we healed everything that did not look like Heaven? What if our goal was to allow Heaven on Earth as promised?

As the frequency, or vibration, increases and the magnetics decrease, some people will choose to stay in the denser, more material world, without spirit. They may have a very difficult time. The merging of science and spirit may be too much of a paradigm shift. They may be fearful and angry as the world drastically changes. And it will continue to change. It always has. We see it in our weather, in new diseases, and in changing economies. For those of us whose focus is the Light and the Oneness of the ALL, we can be lovingly present, filled with compassion. As a part of the Oneness, we understand the fear and the anger of others.

I am on a healing journey to raise my vibration, to unencumber myself of the old wounds, aches and pains, so that the Light flows easily through my body. Whether or not we have dramatic Earth changes and economic disasters, it will make no difference, for I will be in the right place at the right time doing the right thing, in line with the Divine. I am learning to accept peace and joy as a way of life. I have come to Earth with purpose.

Whether the Light comes in the form of a photon belt or a gradual shift in electromagnetics, it is an exciting time! As Klein indicated, now is the time to make the quantum leap into higher consciousness, into higher dimensions. We can assist the process by preparing ourselves and thus enhancing our transformations. On this sacred, healing journey while on the Earth, we can learn to live in peace, even in the middle of chaos. As with the Divine Creator's promise, we can bring Heaven to Earth with our love and compassion.

THE HEALING JOURNEY

*Someday, after we have mastered the winds,the waves, the tides
and gravity, we shall harness for God the energies of love.*
*Then for the second time in the history of the world,
man will have discovered fire.*
Teilhard de Chardin

Healing ourselves allows more space within for
light, love and joy. It is a useful journey, regardless of
our philosophical viewpoints. For many, it is a sacred
journey. If we are truly a part of the One, then any
healing we do for ourselves also heals the ALL. Now, in
the midst of chaos, is the time to work on integration
with our higher self, to not feel separate from God or
from our true self. Now is the time to make way for the
fire of God. Now is the time to fill ourselves with the
Light and Love of the Divine Creator, to heal ourselves
while on Earth.

I am in a holotropic breath workshop,
sitting still in a slightly altered state, listening to Jackie Small, author and workshop
leader, talk about "willingness."

I imagine myself standing firmly with feet apart, arms overhead, and reaching up and out to the Heavens. I notice a revolving Earth has settled behind me. It is a beautiful image. I am enjoying the wanderings of my imagination. I look out to the Universe and repeat Jackie's words: *I am willing! I am willing!*

A flash of lightning sears through my body. I explode into a trillion pieces and watch as tiny bits of my body are instantly scattered throughout the blackness of the Universe. I have disintegrated! I look between two halves of the Earth. I have ceased to exist. My God, I have ceased to exist! Waves of terror wash over me. I am lost in the blackness of space.

But in the next instant I know I am the ALL of the Universe. As I look out through every tiny scattered bit of me, I am everywhere at once. I know everything, experience everything through each tiny piece. I know, I know. Nothing and everything — it is the same! I feel incredible peace. I am everything and everywhere.

Tiny parts of my self begin to gather themselves together from the far reaches of the Universe. I am whole and the Earth is again behind me.

Jackie has finished speaking. I leave the session to walk in the woods. Something strange and wonderful has just happened. I need to integrate.

The wise one within, that all-knowing, all-seeing voice inside, is the part that offers us freedom from our fears, our worries, our separateness. It is the true self that was present at birth, before the learned self. It is our inner wisdom that comes from our contact with a Higher Power, however each of us defines that. When we are connected and aware of the wise self, we know peace. We can walk through chaotic times with this inner sense of peace, dealing with whatever stuff comes our way. We do not live in fear. We enter willingly and joyfully into life, with all its conflict and chaos. We understand our family, our friends, our communities, the animals, the birds, the trees, the flowers, and the Universe. We are connected to the ALL and we are one with it. We live as one. We know all. We are love and compassion. The energy of the Universe flows unencumbered through us. Thought creates. We ask and we receive. It is as simple as that.

However, not all of our earthly experiences support such a truth. When we entered our earthly bodies, with their great density, we forgot. We learned to believe in struggle and hard work. Such was the case for me. Mostly I just plugged along, trying to make sense of my world, often just licking my wounds, but not knowing how to heal them, so that I would not repeat the cycles. But now is the time of quantum healing, of instant change — and for the whole Universe. For if we are ONE, then when we heal ourselves, we heal the ALL. What you do for you, you do for another. Your own healing is a gift. So ask yourself: *Am I willing to be healthy and whole, to be a Light Being in body on Earth, to be all that I can be.* In a loving and gentle manner, notice the internal dialogue that responds to your own *I am willing* statement.

In my counseling practice, clients come to me with a variety of complaints and issues. Some come for marriage counseling; some come for divorce counseling. Others are referred by physicians because of physical complaints that range from headaches to cancer. Some are depressed, lonely, or filled with fear. Some are discouraged with their jobs. Some have insufficient money. Others have been physically and sexually abused. All are searching.

Before undertaking a healing journey, one must be willing to change. Not everyone is willing to enter into the experience of change; it is unknown and the unknown is often difficult for us to deal with. We are rewarded for our traumas, even if we are unaware of the reward. Sometimes we find comfort in our pain. In a loving and gentle manner, ask yourself what you get from difficult situations. Notice, without blaming or judging yourself, how many of your daily conversations are about what is *not* working for you. What would you talk about if life was just as you desired? Do you *know* what you desire?

I ask clients: *How will you know when therapy is finished?* I often receive vague, unclear responses. We become stuck in the image of lack and of pain. We lose the image of how it would be if all were as we desired. We have an image of what we do not want and are living in that reality. We need to awaken from the slumber of our own pain and start to create a new reality! We have the gift of free will — choice. First, we need an awareness that our current reality is a choice! Then, we need to choose.

If I could grant you your wishes for a perfect life, what would that be for you? Think about it as if there were no limitations.

Would it be:

- all the money you desire;
- ideal relationships with significant others, family, friends;
- an enjoyable and energized career;
- good health and great energy;
- love;
- success;
- trust of your inner wise self.

Healing Option

Continue with your own list. Brainstorm as many ideas as you can. What are your desires? Be outrageous. Go for the gold!

If all your wishes and desires were granted, would you be willing to live that way, free of your limitations and embracing all the delights of life on Earth? Now pick one of your desires. Say to yourself "*I am willing to have _____, to be _____.*"

Then, without any blame or judgement, notice any resistance you have to that *I am willing* statement. Look for any 'yabuts' that live over your shoulder, just out of range of your consciousness. Listen carefully as you continue to repeat your desires to yourself. Clues for your healing work lie in being aware of the resistance to a new reality. By paying attention to our own responses, we begin to understand our internal healing journey.

If you are willing, if you truly desire another life reality, to live in the Light, then come with me while we explore a few of the different ways of healing, through the wisdom that lies within you.

Life as Illusion

I remember when I first read *Illusions* by Richard Bach. Some of my friends thought it was a story about airplanes. I thought it was a story about life.

I used to think the Earth was solid and then I rode the waves of an earthquake. I used to think knowing was limited to the five senses and then I traveled to the far reaches of the Universe. I used to think a rock was solid and then I discovered the energy of the atom. I used to look for the right way and then I discovered the truth of many ways.

Once we understand that life is an illusion and that we have had a great hand in the creation of that illusion, we gain tremendous power. However, we also must take on the responsibility for our creations.

But what about the abuse by my parents, you may ask. My spouse is an alcoholic. He drinks, not me. The car ran into my house. I did not ask for it to run into my house. How can I be responsible for creating that? Notice how the mind resists the idea of our part in the creation of our reality, especially the stuff we do not like.

If, for now, it creates too much stress, too much resistance, to think you have a hand in everything in your life, think about some of the things you might be willing to accept some ownership in: an argument with a parent; a conflict with a boss; the stress headache; or your financial situation.

We may disagree about who created what, but the first key to the wise self lies in the response to the situation. Would you believe you have complete power over how you respond to any given situation? ANY SITUATION!!!

Our thoughts, our emotions, our body — they are one. It is not necessary that a real world exist to create a body response. We saw that with the imagined lemon. But let's try that again. Come join me.

Imagine I have taken you to the high desert for a camping trip. It is breathtakingly beautiful. As the sun goes down, we choose to sleep in the open on the earth so that we can watch the wonders of the heavens as the night unfolds. The night is cool, but our down sleeping bags will keep us snug and warm. We slip off to sleep as a full moon glides across the heavenly expanse of stars.

You awaken to the sun touching the tops of the distant mountain peaks. The warmth of the rays feels good on your face. Coffee would taste good, but for now you snuggle within, against the still cool morning desert air. As you start to stretch a bit, you suddenly feel something slowly slither up one side of your leg towards your stomach. Your body stiffens. Your heart starts to pound. You will your heart to be still, but it ignores you.

I look over at you and call out for you to shake a leg and get the coffee on. I start toward you. Beads of perspiration form on your brow. Your eyes shine with terror. You silently mouth the words, *No, No!* I stop and notice a rattlesnake's head peeking out next to your chin. The snake moves over your neck and settles in the morning sun next to your shoulder.

STOP!

Notice your body, your emotions. If you are like many of my workshop participants, your hands are tingling or sweaty; your body is tight and tense; your breathing has almost stopped. You may feel some lightheadedness. Your stomach may be flip-flopping. Notice the sensations in your body. You may be feeling fearful.

STOP! THERE IS NO SNAKE. Take a slow, deep breath. Shake those sensations out of your body. YOU ARE NOT IN THE DESERT! Hello multiple reality! While sitting, reading this, you were also in a desert. Interesting.

Many of my friends have told me that the western *Lonesome Dove* was a great television mini-series. I do not know because I could not get past the snake scene in the first episode. For those of you who did not see the series, the snake scene is powerful. A young man is terrified of crossing the river with the cattle drive. The tension mounts as all the cowboys and the entire herd of cattle reach the other side, leaving the young man on the opposite river bank. Ultimately, he must cross or be left behind. With intense fear and trepidation he starts across on his horse. Halfway into the river, the water explodes. Swarms of snakes, rousted out by the crossing cattle, attack him and his horse. The water is alive with masses of killing snakes. The young cowboy dies, his greatest fear realized. Shaking, I shut off the television!

Ah, the power of the mind! This pretend story on the television has become real in my thoughts, emotions, body sensations and behaviors. Simultaneously, I have been in my living room and also in the river.

A long time ago, I ran across a saying: "Some of the things that will live longest in my memory never really happened." Often our reality lives only in our mind.

One morning your boss walks by your desk and says *Stop by my office before you leave tonight!* Of course, your first thought is *Oh, I bet she is going to give me a raise!* Right? Wrong! Normally, we would go right to *I wonder what I did wrong.*

You are not invited to a party but everyone you know has been invited. You respond *My invitation must have gotten lost in the mail.* Right? Wrong! Usually we start fussing. We go right to fear, blame or worry. Our body goes right to stewing in its own juices, stomach becomes upset, muscles tighten, headaches creep up over the neck and down the shoulders.

True, all of us have issues we have to deal with, but most of us worry about things that have not yet happened. We spend much of our mind time either fretting over the past or worrying about the future. We create and structure our lives by the illusions we create in our imagination and then behave as if they were true. Such illusions live long in our memory, even though they did not actually happen.

When we finally get to talk to our boss or see our friend about the party, we are already upset. And nothing has happened yet. A creation of our mind, an illusion, has become our reality in our body, in our thoughts, and in our emotions.

We can be amused at these scenarios, but our lives are full of the scenarios of our imagination, of the many realities — past, present or future. And the body responds to all of them as if they were true.

The first step in our healing journey is to start noticing, without blame or judgement, our thoughts, our emotions, and our body responses. Be very kind to yourself as you begin your healing journey.

Healing Option

Commit yourself to lovingly and gently observing for just 24 hours how many of your thoughts are fussings about the past or worries about the future. Begin by noticing your emotions and the aches and pains in your body. They will be clues to the self talk of your illusions. Make some notes on your 24-hour noticing experience.

Your thoughts, your emotions and your aches and pains will begin to bring to your awareness how your unconscious experience creates your current reality.

The good news is, if we are creating illusions, then we can create new illusions as we desire!

CREATING REALITIES
WITH LIVING AFFIRMATIONS

We sit in prayer, facing the altar. The Buddhist teacher encourages us to chant for whatever we desire. He encourages one to chant for the $1000 he needs; another to chant for a compatible roommate; another for a school loan; another for a car. Week after week, we chant to meet our material needs. We pray for *things*.

Each week, as we gather together, we take a little time to share the manner in which those requests have been manifested in our everyday lives. Finally, the teacher agrees to respond to our inquires about chanting for *things*. We seek Spiritual enlightenment. Chanting for material things does not seem very spiritual, especially for those of us who grew up thinking that deprivation was the road to Heaven.

The teacher smiles. Quietly he says, *Once you know that you can always bring into your life everything you desire, you no longer need to desire those things. They are yours as you think them. The mind is then free to welcome in Spirit.*

Webster defines affirm as "to assert strongly." Consciously or unconsciously, every moment of our life, we are affirming. Life is just a series of affirmations. Unfortunately, much of my past affirming, at the unconscious level, was negative and not very useful. The computer of my mind has been deeply programmed by my environment and experience. I am now getting in my life the sum of my unconscious thoughts — and I have thousands of daily unconscious thoughts!

As children we accepted what we were told and what we were told became a part of us. This does not mean we have to blame others for our thoughts. It just means we want to bring thoughts about the past events to awareness and effectively and efficiently deal with them, to let them go or to heal them. As adults we can choose — if we are aware. When you start listening to yourself you will be amazed at what your self has unconsciously been saying. Every thought, conscious or unconscious, *is* an affirmation. The goal is to become aware of the unconscious thoughts or affirmations and then create thoughts, or affirmations, more useful in our lives.

Some of my clients are resistant to creating affirmations, to chanting for *things*. They tell me they do not believe affirmations work. I think they ALWAYS work IF, and it is a big IF, the person works with the affirmations.

Rote affirmations do not always work due to our internal balance system. Imagine yourself as a teeter-totter. On your left hand is stacked every negative thought you had about a particular situation; on your right hand is stacked the new affirmation. (See figure 1)

The left side is practically hitting the floor under the weight of all those past messages; the right side, with a few rote affirmations, is in the air. There is no balance between the two. A few rote affirmations have no chance against hundreds of ingrained negative thoughts. Those old messages are very powerful.

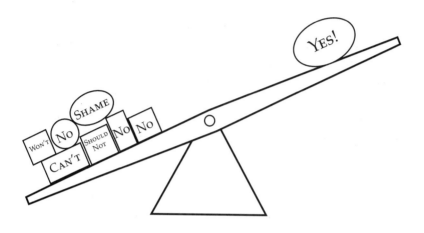

FIGURE 1

Rote repetition of an affirmation often does not result in the dramatic healing life changes you may desire, even if you repeat the affirmation twenty times a day. If what you are doing is meeting an internal need, even if it is an old, outdated message, you will continue to repeat the situation, until the internal need is healed. As you listen to your internal dialogue, you will know what needs to be healed for the new reality to be created. You will also always know what needs healing by the things you desire (for example, money, happiness, peace) and are not getting, or by the things you have and do not want (for example, depression, physical pain, bad relationship). Be kind to yourself. We generally live the way we do because we do not know what else to do.

However, affirmations are one of the quickest ways to get to the root of what is interfering with your having what you desire. The goal is to heal life issues, so that the mindful wise self is ever more present, guiding your earthly body to more peace and joy.

After affirmations become an integral part of your daily healing, you will begin to notice that you no sooner think something and it becomes so. Heaven on Earth. It *can* be that simple, but most of us have been programmed for hard work. If something is of value, we believe we must suffer or struggle to gain or achieve it. Imagine how it would be if the opposite were true — if life was easy.

Working at the computer on this chapter, my fingers type *Life is easy! Life is easy!* Suddenly, I am aware my body has gone crazy. My head shakes *No! No!* My right shoulder hunches forward and my head slouches down. My body spasms and stiffens. Throughout my whole body I am getting *No, no. Life is hard. Nothing in life is easy. Life is hard!* I smile. Such resistance! And I had thought I had come so far in my journey. H'mm. True, but still a ways to go. And this affirmation, at the body-mind level, just gave me another hint about my unfinished tasks. My fingers may be typing *Life is easy!* but my body is saying *No, No, No.*

The goal of living affirmations is to discover what parts of yourself disagree with the affirmation.

Heal those parts, those old wounds. Release the energy ties to old information and open up space for your desires.

As you say your affirmation, listen to the old self talk and pay attention to your body. When there is no resistance in the body or the mind, the affirmation becomes reality, and life becomes more peaceful.

The following is my living affirmation therapeutic process: awareness, attention and action. I call it my AAA process.

AWARENESS:

To begin the healing process of affirmations, I ask myself *What do I want?* or *What do I want more of?* You may want more money, a loving relationship, a change in business, good health, high energy, or more time to relax. Figuring out what you want can be very challenging and may take some time and effort. We are often unaware of the specifics of our desires.

A word of caution: the more clear you are (i.e., more unencumbered energy flowing though you), the more quickly your affirmation is realized. It is important to be very clear with the intention and with the language. You get what you ask for — literally. The Universe treats a request just as a computer treats information.

Begin by taking a minute and just brainstorming about some things you might want. Focus on desired outcome. Pick one outcome.

I decided *I want more money.*

What do you want? As if you are the writer, director and producer of a play, create in your imagination the desired scenario in vivid, living color. Be personal; use the present tense; be action-oriented. Create a living play. What are you doing? What are others doing? What are you saying? What are others saying? What are you feeling? Others feeling? Keep changing the play until it meets all aspects of your desired outcome. In your imagination, experience the living affirmation.

I see lots of money just raining down on me. It really feels good. Jim likes it a lot, but I'm not sure others are as happy for me. H'mmm?

Now, create a short verbal affirmation that instantly brings the "play" into your own experience. This is an affirmation you will say out loud so that, with sound, you begin to co-create.

More money is coming into my life.

What is your short verbal affirmation?

As you create your affirmations, use present tense statements (*I am* _____ instead of *I am "going to"*) otherwise you will always be "going to." Use positive statements. The 'not' statements are confusing for the Universe and often get programmed as positive statements. For example, *I will not eat that piece of cherry pie in the refrigerator* just brings up images of cherry pie. Try, instead: *I desire healthy foods that are good for my body.*

ATTENTION:

Now, be the loving and non-judgmental observer just attending to the issues that come up. Be gentle and kind with yourself. As you repeat the short version of your affirmation to yourself, pay attention to the little voices that come to sabotage your affirmation — the yabuts. I appreciate the yabuts for they provide healing information.

Notice any internal negative responses that interfere with an image becoming truth for you: thoughts, body responses, feelings, etc. Let that stream of consciousness just roll with your yabuts.

Notice also how you rewarded yourself for not having your affirmation. An example is good health. Think how we reward ill health. How many times do people call in to the workplace to say *Hey, I won't be in today because I am feeling healthy!* People create headaches, sore throats, whatever they told themselves when they got up in the morning and decided not to go to work. In our work environments we reward the very behavior we do not wish to have. Be kind to yourself in your noticing, for the external environment has often rewarded you for trauma and drama.

Great! I just noticed if I think more money, I think more work. Not a good idea. I change my affirmation to:

More money is easily coming into my life.

Now, I notice that I think I do not deserve that. So I change it to:

More money is easily coming into my life. I deserve it.

Oops! Still doesn't feel good. When I say that, I think of the verse: It's harder for a rich man to get into

43

Heaven than for a camel to get through the eye of a needle.

Great! Long-standing Protestant message there. While channel surfing, I notice on PBS a picture of the eye of the needle. It is a rock formation! Camels had to get on their knees to get through. Not impossible, just needs attention.

So, I add:

I deserve it and appreciate it. <u>I will use it for the good of others and for the good of myself.</u>

This feels a little better, but it still does not feel totally comfortable.

More money is easily coming into my life, <u>as in line with the Divine</u>. I deserve it and I appreciate it. I will use it for the good of others and for the good of myself.

Feels much better.

I can now see my affirmation in living color, say it out loud, and feel it as if it could be true; that is, all my 'yabuts' seem to be satisfied.

As you say your affirmation to yourself, what do you notice?

ACTION:

The first action step is to repeatedly say your affirmation out loud. Continue to notice any yabuts and alter the affirmation accordingly. It is important to say it often to start countering all the old messages piled up on the negative side of the teeter-totter.

Sometimes when I say my new affirmation, an old message comes into my awareness. I have several options for what to do with these old messages. First, I need to decide if the message holds any truth for me. It may be an old parental message and all I need do is let go of it, to consciously choose to no longer have the old message be a part of my thought pattern.

I can also create a pattern interruption, if just letting go does not seem sufficient to break the old affirmation. One example would be with my money affirmation. When it feels too difficult to break the pattern, I can interrupt the old message. I just remind myself about the camel, or I may remind myself how much good I can do for others with my money.

Sometimes I want an instant pattern interruption. One of my favorites is the Light scan. In my imagination I see Light moving down from the Heavens through my head, out my hands and out my feet and down into the Earth, clearing and cleansing everything in the path. It is a powerful pattern interruption, especially for emotions. And it only takes a moment.

Another instant pattern interruption is a deep belly breath. I am always amazed at how much stuff disappears if I breathe out the unwelcome thoughts and emotions. Rather than holding my breath and locking the emotions into my emotional holding pot in my belly, I take a deep, relaxing breath, filling my belly with full breath. I then gently exhale, relaxing and moving the thoughts and emotions out of my body. What instant pattern interruption is useful for you?

The second action step is to ask myself what small step could I take to help me meet my goal. Do I need to return a phone call, get my bills out, or work on my book? Sometimes procrastination can be a wonder-

ful personal behavior area in which to develop
affirmations.

Healing Option

Take some time to develop an affirmation for
healing yourself. Lovingly notice the yabuts and keep
alert for the healing information. Notice when you say
your affirmation how your body responds. Keep listening to yourself and fine-tuning your affirmation until
all parts of your self believe.

Try repeating your affirmations for twenty-one
days. Start noticing the changes in your life! It is so
much fun to be a co-creator in life.

As you gradually develop your living
affirmations for all aspects of your life, you will notice
that many of your past issues are healed and are no
longer important. Life is changing, becoming easier and
more peaceful. You become the architect of your life;
you are creating new realities with your thoughts and
actions. Your challenge is to ask yourself what you
want.

Mirror, Mirror on the Wall

He said *Get a sawhorse and lie down backwards on it. Then the severe pain in your neck and shoulders will go away.* He seemed to be a bit of a crazy old man. I ignored him.

Years later I am at my parent's farm. There in the tool shed sits an old sawhorse. I remember the weird comments by the strange man in Vermont.

I notice the pain in my neck and shoulders. It lives with me constantly. I think *What the heck! Why not?*

I pull the sawhorse into an open area in the shed. Not exactly sure how to lie back on it, I straddle the sawhorse, letting my shoulders rest back into the long wooden spine.

Oh God! Screams fill my mind. *No! No! Don't! Stop! Please, stop!* My body is filled with rage. I want to pound. I want to hit. I want to kill.

I sense horses off to my right. I smell hay.

I roll off the sawhorse. On my knees, head buried in my hands, body shaking, I sob. I stiffen. Someone might hear me. I take a couple of short breaths and pull myself together. I wipe my eyes, straighten my body, and stuff the pain within.

I have no idea what just happened, but it will be a cold day in hell before I try that again!

I put the sawhorse away. Composed, I walk back into my parent's house. Twenty years pass before I have the courage to revisit the unnamed rage.

For much of my life, one of my best survival methods was to deny, to pretend all was well. Severe sinus infections, debilitating migraines, and walking with a cane when the back pain grew too great were normal parts of my life. I lived disconnected from my body as much as possible, traveling to far away places in my mind to escape the emotional and physical pain. And then it became too painful not to be home in my body.

Another of my great roles was martyr, to smile and suffer in silence. I was a reactor, not an actor in my world. That role is no longer useful, but it was an easy mask for many years. I wore many masks: nice girl; strong woman; tough cookie; always right; always brave.

On rare occasions — about once every five years — I would explode, ranting, raving and blaming. When hurt is not resolved, anger, anxiety, fear and sadness build up, living in a pot of emotions in the midsection of the body. The lid must be kept tightly clamped on. It takes a great deal of energy to keep the pot intact. Oh, once in a while I let off a little steam, a bit of sarcasm here and there, leaking the pain out onto my family and friends. Maybe I had a bit of relief, but I quickly slipped my nice girl mask back on. I needed ways to clean out the pot and tools that would help me keep it cleaned out.

Hundreds of self-help books and workshops helped me discover that I am responsible for what I feel and do. My emotions are learned responses. I used to project those emotions out into the world with he/she statements: *He makes me so angry.* Or *If she would be a little more considerate, I would be happier.* Belief that another has the power to make us healthy, happy and whole robs us of our own power and control. If I listen to myself complain, I hear my projections. My goal is to listen to myself and to continually search for healthy ways to reclaim my projections — and my power.

I have learned that no one can emotionally hurt me unless I give them the power to do so. Outside events have no such power. Any emotion I experience is but a reflection of my unfinished business, a mirror in the outside world. It does not mean that I have to like some of the negative "stuff' that happens out there, nor does it excuse another's behavior. It only means I can choose how I *respond* to the "stuff." I may still need to problem solve behaviors in ongoing relationships, but first I want to take care of my own emotional baggage.

I now live with two life assumptions:

First, my external world is a direct reflection of my internal state. As if looking into a mirror, I can see what areas of my life still need healing. Whatever is manifested in my world is direct feedback, as long as I am willing to look.

Second, I may have no control over what you do. However, I have the ability to choose the way I feel and respond to what you do. That ability will be in direct correlation to my own awareness. Whether I feel sad, glad, mad, afraid, guilty or jealous, the emotions are mine and are related to my past experiences. What I do is based on how I learned to respond to past situations. I will continue to feel and to respond in like manner until I bring my responses into consciousness and turn them into choices.

These two assumptions are the basis of the physical and emotional healing that I do, for myself and with my clients. What I am feeling and what is happening in my environment mirrors back to me the status of my healing journey.

When we are born, we coo when we are satisfied. We cry when hungry, wet or afraid. Then, hopefully, someone comes and feeds us, changes us or reassures us. As we grow older others may start telling us how and what we feel; how and what to do; and how and what to think. Others may say they love us but then turn away. They do not respond to our every need. We begin to feel separate, isolated and lonely. Telling the truth is not always rewarded. Not telling the truth feels strange in our bodies so we begin to shut out the body information from our awareness. In order not to feel the hurt, we add on layer after layer of armor. We get farther away from our truth. Others are not telling the truth either, so everyone is in a guessing game. Based on our own fears, we create scenarios in our head.

As adults, much of the time we are no longer present in awareness. We are anticipating problems of the future or reliving the experiences of the past. People no longer automatically understand us or knowingly meet our needs. We feel hurt, sad, angry, guilty, afraid or jealous and want them to guess what is going on. We want them to satisfy our needs. Time and time again we are disappointed. Our greatest disappointments are our unmet expectations. What we want we either think they should know *or* we are so far away from our truth, we do not really know what we want.

Instead of our bodies responding to the dangers in the outside world, our bodies are most often responding to the dangers of our internal creations. Since the body does not know the difference between what happened and what the mind is thinking, the body responds in fight-flight mode to our thoughts. Since we usually do not fight or flee on a regular basis, we, again, armor our emotions up in our bodies, layer by layer, storing it for some future leaking or pot dumping.

When I bring related information to consciousness, my feelings change. So once I know my learned thoughts result in my feelings and body responses, I can search my history. I can then change how I feel about my history. I observe what occurred and, with insight, I can change my thoughts and thus my feelings about it. Sometimes, as a form of therapy, I may exaggerate what I am feeling or what my body is experiencing. Then I ask myself how this experience is familiar, or similar, to past events. I often discover a pattern I have had for years. Once I become aware, I have choices about how I respond.

As a barometer, I have learned that if an emotion lasts more than fifteen minutes, I probably need to look deeper within myself. For the big stuff, such as death of a loved one, divorce, job loss, or trauma, I give myself longer times of healing. If I seem stuck, or I have a big pot of emotions to heal, I will probably see a therapist, for some assistance on moving through the emotions of my experience, or cleaning out the pot. With the new healing techniques, such as Eye Movement Desensitization and Reprocessing (EMDR) and Thought Field Therapy (TFT), even the big emotional experiences can get processed in a short amount of time. These new techniques quickly healed the old pain in my shoulders and the terror I remembered when I climbed onto that sawhorse in my parent's tool shed.

As I get older, I find I have a lower tolerance for frustration and discomfort. If the chaotic world is mirroring unfinished business, then I want to take a look at it and get it resolved so I can get back to joy and peace. I do want more joy and peace.

After I have done my internal observing and healing of a particular emotional experience (about 80-90% of the stuff), I can now address any of the unresolved, external relationship issue (about 10-20% of the stuff) related to that experience. Many of my relationship problems are really just symptoms, or mirrors, of *my* unfinished business. Often the healing of my emotions is sufficient for me to find peace.

So first I have awareness (I feel emotional, can't get a thought out of my head, or my body hurts), then understanding (I notice an old pattern, an old message, or a forgiveness needed) and then I take action for my own healing. It is the taking action that will keep the pot from rebuilding.

If it is still a relationship issue, I may need to ask myself *What am I not saying or doing that I need to be saying or doing?* After I have figured out the relationship issue, I need to figure out a way to address that issue in a loving and gentle manner. For me, that means figuring out my truth, gently speaking it, listening to their truth, and then problem solving with the other person.

A rule of thumb in conflict management is that if

a person is emotional they will not respond to logic. That is true for me; that is true for the other person. So it just makes sense to first deal with my emotional issues and then go to problem solving.

To keep the pot from rebuilding, I ask myself what I would have liked to have done or said in the first place. For me, a lot of my pot of emotions gets created because I do not speak truth. As I become more aware of what is happening within me, I then can report that to another person as my truth. I can describe their behavior as a part of my experience, but my truth is my responsibility. For example, if you are curt on the phone with me (or so I believe), it would only create defensiveness if I told you I thought you were curt. Then we would probably argue. But if instead I just described my experience, it might be easier for us to problem solve. Therefore, I might say to you *When I was talking to you on the phone yesterday, I wasn't sure you were hearing me and I am wondering if I said something to upset you, something that would create some distance between us.* Then I need to be quiet and listen to what you say. Notice I have just relayed my perceptions. You might have a totally different experience. If, however, I had complained to you about not ever listening to me, you probably would have gotten defensive and we would have both been in emotion. It may be that your mind was just somewhere else, or it may be that you were irritated with me, in which case my perception may be true and we need to problem solve.

If I do not problem solve the relationship issues, I will keep getting them mirrored back to me in a variety of formats. I can divorce one man because he drinks, but if I do not resolve my internal issues, heal my internal, emotional pot, I will probably just marry another man who drinks, or find a boss who drinks. I always know the status of my healing by the mirror of my external situations.

So let's revisit the assumptions:

First, my external experience is a direct reflection — a mirror — of my internal state. I can look out and know what areas of my life still need healing. Whatever is manifested in my world is direct feedback, as long as I am willing to look.

Second, I may have no control over what you do. However, I have the ability to choose the way I feel and respond to what you do.

I know my feelings are really my feelings. I take ownership and responsibility for them. My happiness truly comes from within. As I do my internal healing I notice that the external world is reflecting a much more peaceful face. Now I know that what originally seemed to be a problem is a blessing in disguise. My family, my friends, my co-workers or strangers can all be blessings for me in the disguise of problems. I call them my angel blessings for they show up for my healing work.

Sometimes it is very difficult to find the blessing side of a situation. When I got divorced, I thought the world would end. I was devastated. However, it was a turnaround time in my life. I was a secretary and that was okay, but it was not my life purpose. Now, I am a counselor/consultant. I am doing just what I love to do. I needed a really good angel kicking in the backside to get me going. And I am grateful. Be aware; it's hard to see these angel blessings for they often come with really good disguises.

The goal of the mirror is to reflect back the little "stuff" of life before it turns into huge, black pits of crisis and chaos. As we get better at looking into the mirror of life, at noticing the reflections of our unfinished business, we can more quickly address the lessons we find there and return to a more peaceful journey.

Healing Option

Take a moment and, without blame and judgment, examine yourself and your external world. What is being reflected back to you? What is happening in your life that you wish was not happening? Who are your angel blessings in disguise?

Listen carefully to how you describe "others" who are not behaving as you would prefer they do. These very words are your own healing challenges. For example, you might think your spouse is not very understanding. How is "understanding" an issue for you? Do you need to be more understanding or are you too understanding? You are the detective; the clues are in your world and in the way you describe your world.

In our healing journey, the world is our mirror; life is an illusion and we are the creators of our realities. What power we have over our life experiences! Now is the time to attend to your life situations, to that emotional, chaotic stuff, so that unencumbered Light energy can more easily flow through you and you can experience more peace and joy. It is time to heal the unfinished business, to become conscious. Heal all that is not of Heaven for you are on Earth with purpose.

BEING A LIGHT WORKER

A vision without a task is but a dream,
a task without a vision is drudgery,
a vision and a task is the hope of the world.
— From a church in Sussex, England, c 1730

The difference between a Light Worker and a Light Being is intention and action. All are Light Beings and all will be in the Light. When and how are the questions for each of us. The planet Earth is ascending; we are ascending. We can do this easily and with joy; we can be intentional Workers of Light and assist the process, or we can just hang around and let it happen to us. To me, it seems an easier journey if I proceed with intention and action. It means healing the old wounds, opening up space within myself for the Light and then moving forward with purpose and consciousness. It means that even in the middle of this changing, chaotic world, I live in peace.

As Light Workers, we walk with intention and action. Brooke Medicine Eagle offered three preparation options for this Shift of the Ages. One is <u>contemplation</u>. Webster defines contemplation as "to meditate on; to regard thoughtfully; to intend; to think over carefully." For me, contemplation is paying attention to the present moment, to the experience of the now. I pay attention and honor the food I eat; I feel the joy of the Earth as a rose glistens with a drop of morning dew; I offer gratitude for the blessings of home and family; I take a walk and enjoy feeling the Earth beneath my feet; I cry with joy at the birth of a baby; I pray for those in need and in pain. I contemplate my life on Earth as I live this very moment. Staying in the now keeps me from spending time in the trauma and drama of yesterday or in creating worries about the unknowns of tomorrow.

Being in the present moment also means noticing, without blame and judgment, when I become emotional or feel physical pain. Then, I take action by attending to the situation and by taking the time to heal the emotional and physical pains. I then become a clear conduit for the magnificent Light of Spirit — for myself and for the Earth.

Never in modern history have there been so many Light Workers — people who consciously contemplate the situation, who offer prayers, who thoughtfully meditate on the experience of the now and who take action in line with the Divine.

Another of Brooke Medicine Eagle's action options is meditation into non-material realms. It is the reason I have included my non-material journeys in this writing. Traveling in the space of our mind, in that non-material state, is practice — for life and for death. We are moving to the still point, the veil point, that zero point, of space where we experience multiple realities of our choice. The veil between Heaven and Earth is thinner.

I love science fiction. Our children seem prepared for multiple realities. They have had oodles of Saturday morning cartoon experiences of morphing, of strange beings, and of strange experiences. We, as adults, seem to get stuck in thinking there is only one way to be. The non-material state offers us opportunities to experience multiple realities, which we can learn to control. Remember control? It is that thing so important to us Earthlings.

Another goal of meditating in the non-material space is to confront unfinished business. Our fears and issues will show up there in our imaginations, just as they do in this reality where we live. In our imaginations we can also practice the power of creation. In these non-material altered states, we can learn to be in charge of what we create. It is a place to practice instant manifestation, instant creation!

A client is sitting in my office describing a particularly horrifying dream. It had been a life-long repeater.

The night is cold and dark. The street is empty. The shadows are long and distorted. My client hears footsteps echoing in the lonely streets. Over his shoulder he sees a figure in a black, hooded robe.

My client hastens his steps and then, fearfully, breaks into a run. The hooded figure follows.

He awakens, heart pounding, hands sweaty and stomach in knots. My client is too terrified to return to sleep.

In my office I have him take a few deep breaths and return to the dream state until he is running and running. This time, I suggest he stop, turn to his chaser and forcefully demand: *What do you want!*

The figure stops and pushes back the hooded cape from his face. A gentle soul says to my client: *I am so glad you asked. I have been chasing* you for a lifetime. I am your protector. I have important news for you . . .

By entering the meditative state, that non-material realm, my client was able to gain a friend, a helper, as well as some valuable insight into life issues. In our dreams, in our meditative states, we can always take charge.

Another of Brooke's action options is <u>service</u>. If we choose to assist humankind we a) make the journey easier and more joyful; and b) assist everyone else to "Lighten Up."

Being compassionate is one way of being of service. Webster defined compassion as "sympathetic consciousness of others' distress together with a desire to alleviate it." Braden wrote that compassion is what you become, not something you do. He also stated that new data suggests that human emotion can impact the patterning of your DNA. It would seem that compassion is not only good for the other, but good for us!

In the Tibetan Buddhist practice of Tonglen you take on, through compassion, all mental and physical sufferings of others (their sadness, fear, grief, pain, anger, guilt and doubt, etc.) and you give them, through your love, the healing of well-being and peace of mind. In *Tricycle*, Fall 1997, Sogyal Rinpoche discussed Tonglen for a dying person. From the Tibetan

Buddhist perspective, you sit in deep meditation/
prayer and invite the transformation and purification of
the one in pain, replacing the pain with ultimate well-
being for the dying person. You, too, are transformed in
the process. Compassion is a way of being, it is action
and it is healing for the ALL.

Once during a typing meditation, when it ap-
peared as if I was getting information new to me, I
asked, *Are you separate from me or are you just me talking
to me?* I was confused. They answered: *Yes.* I chuckled
at the answer. But of course, I am a part of the ALL and
I am a separate human being in the ALL. Both are truth.
As a part of the ALL I have access to the information of
the ALL, although it is distorted by the density and
separateness of my human being. Maybe it does not
matter whom I talk with as long as the information is
useful and encourages the expansion of the wisdom
within my self.

As a part of the One, everything we do affects
the ALL. Thus, if I heal the wounds of my childhood
trauma, or if I choose to be compassionate, or if I choose
to enhance my Light Beingness, I change the vibration
and density of the ALL. I am a Light Worker.

The power of our interrelationships within the
ALL is illustrated by a situation I encountered when I
attended a workshop by Boise chiropractor Dr. Michael
Moriarty.

He asked for three volunteers. He whis-
pered to one, then to another and had them
stand on each side of a third person on
whom he was doing the muscle testing of
applied kinesiology. He tested for strength
and then nodded to the person on the right.

His client tested weak. He nodded to the person on his left. The client tested strong. No words were spoken. The client had no idea why she tested weak and then strong. Michael explained that he had asked the person on the right to think a negative thought about the client when he signaled, and then the person on the left to think a positive thought when he signaled.

Their negative or positive thoughts, with very little or no emotional attachment, created quite a difference in the physical strength of the volunteer client. This is a wonderful example of how our thoughts affect others; of how we are truly interrelated; of how powerful we really are!

If we, in consciousness with clear intention, offer ourselves in service with compassion, if we are aware of our thoughts, if we live in the present moment honoring and healing our pain and being in gratitude for gifts, and if we practice in non-material space the power of focus and creation, we are truly Workers of the Light, clearing the darkness and expanding the space for Light, decreasing the density and increasing the vibration for one and ALL. It is truly a sacred path we walk. As Light Workers, we are the priests and priestess of the Shift of the Ages. Our efforts can assist the Earth and all its inhabitants to more easily be in the Light — to find peace, even in chaotic times.

Healing Option

What forms of contemplation can or do you participate in? Compassion prayers? Attention to the now? Gratitude? What types of non-material states currently offer you creative opportunities? Day dreaming? Night dreams revisited? Meditation? Soul retrieval? What service do you provide? Listening? Caring? Praying? Doing?

As Light Workers, we are conscious of our efforts in helping ourselves and thus helping the ALL. We know that every thought and every action makes a difference. We dedicate ourselves to making a difference, to increasing the peace and joy in the lives of others, as well as in ourselves. We do this in a conscious way, full of awareness of the possibilities of multiple realities.

ENERGETIC CLEARINGS

As I observed my clients, I noticed that much of what they experienced did not even belong to them. Not only did their elders walk around with pots of emotions leaking on them as children, but we as humans walk around leaking our pots of emotions on each other. In my noticing I was reminded of velcro fasteners, for the energy of others seemed to stick like velcro. As a Light Worker, it appears that clearing my energy self is most useful.

Imagining that thought forms are like little bubbles, with emotion and additional thoughts increasing the bubble's dimensions and energy, we can see that thought-emotion bubbles can become powerful. When a person thinks angry or depressed thoughts, their energy is sent outward and affects others. You might have noticed that sometimes you feel angry for no apparent reason, or frustrated, or your body aches. These are clues alerting you to check to see if you have picked up any energy of another which is not useful to your life form.

Healing Angels

During a meditation, I noticed a wonderful angel with a transformational healing basket. I discovered that during compassion prayers for others, I could lift their emotional and physical pain into her basket for transformation to the Light. I could do the same for my own pains. One day in my meditations, I observed that there was "stuff" in my energy field that had yet to reach my physical awareness.

I imagined that the angel had a big comb and was combing through my energy field, taking out any stray energy, any tangles, or any stuckness. This stuff looked like black sticky tar or spider webs strung out or balled up within me. My angel just continued lovingly combing and combing my energy field, from above my head to below my feet, pulling out and putting any undesirable stuff into her transformation basket, all the while smoothing out my energy field. Since it was my mind that had imagined her, I had her also comb through my body to remove any inappropriate energy within my organs, my mental fields, and my emotional fields.

I was amazed at how much stuff I had collected during the day that was not mine. I was also amazed at how much better I felt after this cleansing and smoothing exercise. I realized that I could even ask my angel to clean out old stuff that had leaked into me prior to my awareness, such as in my childhood. When young, we do not know what to do with the anger of an adult that spills out onto us. Often we just take it in and it lives on inside us, leaking out on others. I had lots of anger and sadness living inside me that was not mine. Now it is gone. Sometimes I notice I pick up stuff during my day. My angel is willing to clean out anything that I no longer find useful. See what your angel is willing to do for you!

Healing Option

Close your eyes. Take a few relaxing, deep breaths. Imagine a sacred, healing container — a basket, a box or an urn. Look at yourself with your imaginal eye. If you see any darkness, stickiness, webbing, ask if it is there in your best interest. Trust your intuition. If this stuff is of no use to you, ask that it be removed. You might ask for your own healing angel, or maybe your imagination has another creative idea just for you! What did you notice? What would you change in your next clearing session?

I also have another healing angel who holds a vase full of endless Light and Love. This sparkling energy flows, on my request, into my crown and down through my body, filling up any space cleared and cleansed of old stuff. Any time you make space by healing old stuff, it is important to fill the space with Light so as to not be vulnerable to the leaking energies of others. The healing goal of energetic clearing is to enhance and increase the vibration of your Light energy so that you become a clearer Light Worker.

Not In My Body

Bob White Eagle, a medicine man from New Mexico, came to Idaho to offer teachings about eagle medicine.

In meditation, following a day with him in the Idaho mountains, I saw an eagle streaming toward my face, eyes aflame and

67

claws and beak open in attack mode. Fear engulfed me. I knew I was going to be torn to pieces. Then, the words "Not In My Body" came to mind and I screamed at the eagle *Not in my body!* The eagle passed through the energy field of my body, circled around and settled on my shoulder, where he rides still, a companion and protector.

It was great insight to me, this gift of eagle medicine from White Eagle. I now know that if I am aware of movement into my life form of the energies, the "stuff," of others or of their experiences, I can just say *Not in my body* and it disappears. This allows me to work with others, who are in deep pain, without fear that their stuff will settle within me.

The caretaker of my father was walking down the hall of our house towards me. Her face turned red and became distorted. She angrily screamed at me. The force of her anger pushed me backward and took my breath away. I noticed I wanted to yell right back at her. How dare she say those things to me. She was totally out of line. Quickly, I went into my bedroom and repeated, *Not in my body.* I asked that the anger be transformed so that it would not live in me or in my house. The anger dissipated and I felt calmer. I then walked back into the living room and calmly discussed the caretaker's issues with her.

You will know when an emotion is not yours because it leaves instantly. This also works with physical pain.

I had just spent two 24-hour sleepless shifts with my dying father. He continuously cried out in pain. We thought he might have an ulcer. The caretaker is now with him and we are treating the ulcer.

I am home in my own bed, asleep. Suddenly I can't breathe. I clutch my stomach and roll out of bed onto the floor. The pain is burning in my stomach. I think I will need to have Jim take me to the hospital. I cry out in pain.

Wait! This seems familiar. Is this my pain? Have I picked up my father's pain across time and space? With the pain burning throughout my midsection, I cry out *If this is not my pain, be gone from me!*

I am astonished. I now feel nothing. The intolerable pain of a moment ago has vanished. In awe, I crawl back into bed, wondering what other pains I might have that do not belong to me.

As people become more sensitive they begin to notice that they have headaches or stomach aches or some other symptom similar to someone they know. Ask for an emotion or a pain to leave and, if it is not yours, it will disappear. If it is your emotion or your pain, then one of the other healing options might be more useful, as you experiment in the non-material world. It is a question of noticing what is yours that needs insight and healing or what might be the result of others just leaking their own pain onto you.

Healing Option

Notice any emotions or physical pains. Close your eyes and scan your body in your imaginal mind. Command a desired change and see what happens. Remember to fill any cleared space with Loving Light.

Chakra Clearing, Balancing and Unifying

Literature about the Ascension process encourages chakra clearing, balancing and unifying for improved health and increased energy. The chakra system has existed for thousands of years in Eastern philosophy. There seems to be no definitive source on the chakra system and available literature offers different opinions on the number of chakra points. Most agree, however, that the chakras provide an inter-dimensional system between the physical self and the psychic self. Chakras are often seen by Seers as colored, radiant, spinning spheres of energy.

The experience of being human, and dealing with all our "stuff," seems to clog these energy points. Clearing, balancing and connecting the chakra system provides optimum health. When the major chakras are open, waves of energy, or increased vibration, are often noticed in the physical body. These spheres of energy, or chakras, are capable of being directed by thought. In this exercise, intend that the Light clear each chakra.

For the purpose of this meditation, utilize 11 chakras: (See figure 2, next page)

- An Earth chakra, about 8-10 inches below the feet
- The Feet chakras at the bottom of the feet
- The Omega chakra, about 8 inches below the end of the spine
- The Root chakra at the base of the spine
- The Creative, or sexual, chakra in the area of sexual organs
- The Solar-plexus, or abdomen chakra
- The Heart chakra
- The Throat chakra
- The Third Eye, or forehead, chakra
- The Crown chakra, located in the center at the top of the head
- The Alpha chakra, located 12-15 inches above the top of the head

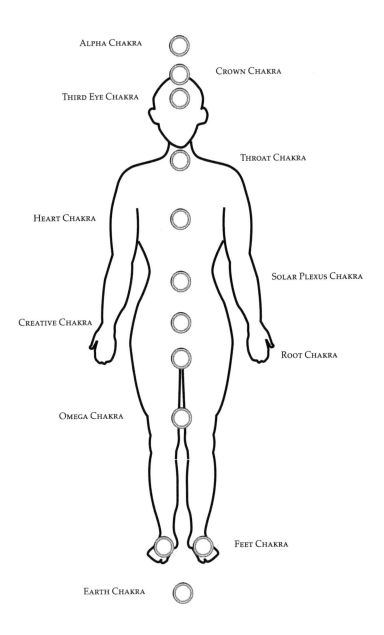

ALPHA CHAKRA

CROWN CHAKRA

THIRD EYE CHAKRA

THROAT CHAKRA

HEART CHAKRA

SOLAR PLEXUS CHAKRA

CREATIVE CHAKRA

ROOT CHAKRA

OMEGA CHAKRA

FEET CHAKRA

EARTH CHAKRA

FIGURE 2

As you use this meditation, insert any minor chakra points where you may be feeling physical discomfort. I have what I refer to as my 4.5 chakra located between my heart and throat. This is my immune system chakra; I am healthier when I keep it open and cleared. Other minor chakras points include the hands, knees, ankles, shoulders, hips, as well as organ points. Be creative in your own healing.

I imagine a sun in the heavens above my head. From the sun drops a ball of Light about the size of a basketball. At the Alpha point, about 12 to 15 inches above my head, this ball of Light splits into four smaller balls, one moving from the single point above me to about a foot behind me, a foot in front, and a foot on each side at the level of my crown chakra. (See figure 3)

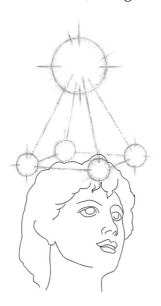

FIGURE 3

These four balls of Light move horizontally back to the center, meeting at my crown chakra and reuniting into one ball of Light that moves back up to the sun. As the four balls of Light move back to the center they fill up the space with Light. As the four combined balls of Light move back to the sun, the path forms a column of Light within the pyramid Light space, cleansing, balancing and connecting the Crown chakra with the Alpha chakra. (See figure 4)

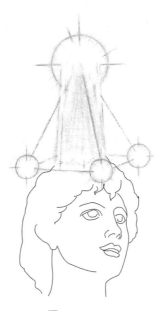

FIGURE 4

Another basketball of Light falls from the sun, splits into four smaller balls at the Alpha point. Each of the four smaller balls of Light again move down the front, sides and back of me to the level of the Third Eye chakra. These four balls of Light again

move horizontally back to the center, meeting in the middle of my head. They return
back to the sun through the center of me,
creating a column of Light through the
center of myself and within the pyramid
space of Light created by the four balls of
Light. This process is clearing, balancing
and unifying the Alpha, Crown and Third
Eye chakras. Looking at me, it would appear as if I had on a pyramid hat of Light.
(See figure 5)

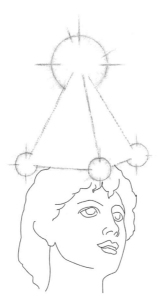

FIGURE 5

I continue this process through each
chakra, including the Earth chakra, bring-
ing the Earth energy and the Heaven energy through the pyramid of Light. The
pyramid of energy has expanded as it
moves through each chakra. The center

column of Light increases in intensity with each passing ball of Light. (See figure 6)

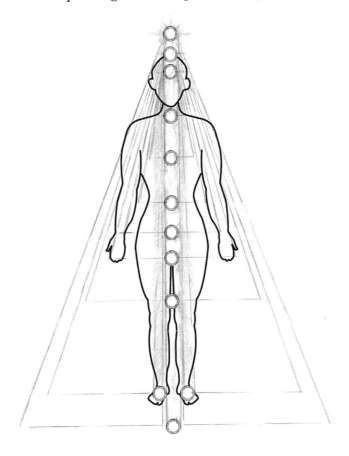

FIGURE 6

After I have created this pyramid of Light, I imagine the energy flowing from the sun, down the pyramid to the energy of the Earth, back up through the center column of Light and then, at the level of the Alpha chakra, spilling out like a fountain of Light energy, back to Earth. This forms a beautiful, rainbow fountain of Light energy that totally surrounds me. (See figure 7)

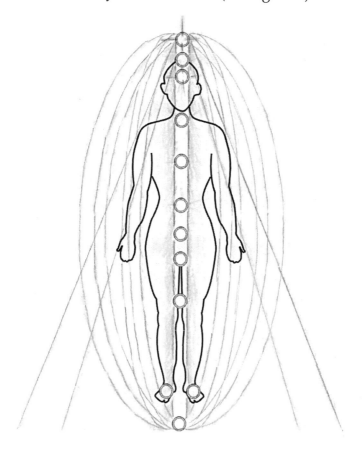

FIGURE 7

This meditation creates a space from which I can safely do my non-material Light Work — for myself and for others.

Entities and Energies

There is much controversy about entities and their realness, but remember we live in a world of multiple realities. Most religions have, or had, rituals for casting our evil. Even Jesus cast out devils. Most of the ascension books have clearing prayers.

Based on my experience and the experience of some of my clients, I believe that energies and entities can attach themselves to us. I believe that there are those who do not accept that they no longer have bodies; I believe that there are those who are aware they do not have bodies but who want to continue to experience life; and I believe there are other things, including bundles of energies, that seem to hang on or around those still living an earthly existence.

Sometimes the Angel's comb is enough to remove unwanted energy from ourselves. But sometimes this is not sufficient. I particularly notice entities hanging on to people who are substance abusers and to people who have been incapacitated for awhile, such as in a hospital. While I do not consider myself in the business of removing entities and bundles of energy, sometimes my clients are in great pain and so we call upon the experts, both of this world and of other worlds.

One prayer that I use seems to be effective:

Oh, Holy Saints and Angels of Love and Light, I ask that you invite all energies and entities that are not in line with the Divine Creator for (name) to a place where they will be met by loved ones and others who will assist them to continue on their spiritual path. Or, if they choose, to return to their origins. Let them be gone from _____ NOW. In the name of all that is Holy, it is so, and I am grateful. Amen, Amen, Amen.

Oh, Holy Saints and Angels of Love and Light, I ask that any space cleared by your work now be filled with Light and Love for the health and wholeness of _____. I ask also that _____ be in perfect alignment with the Divine. In the name of all that is Holy, it is so, and I am grateful. Amen, Amen, Amen.

You can use a similar prayer. Use words that are familiar to you. Any prayer that opens a space should then be followed with a request to have the space filled with Light. The goal of a Light Worker is to create space and allow Light to enter, so that any chaos, any darkness, is transformed in the Light.

Please note that I am not removing anything but, rather, am calling on Higher Powers to do the desired work. As a Light Worker, you need to always get permission, at the Soul level, from other Beings before doing any work with them. The work you do is done as a facilitator for the Soul — for yourself, for the other, for the ALL.

Healing Option

Say a prayer for yourself and notice any differences in your mind or body.

CREATING PERSONAL SACRED SPACE

According to Beck and Metrick in *The Art of Ritual*, creating personal sacred space is a ritual that provides us with a way of using metaphor as a form of intention. Ritual increases balance and connection within ourselves and with others. In line with Quantum Physics, it also connects us with the world and with the movement and energies of the cosmos and the non-material world.

Recently I have noticed an increase in the number of workshops on sacred geometry. Much of the current literature, including Joseph Jockman's *Journeys into Meta-Creation*, uses a sacred geometry approach to provide assistance in understanding Earth changes. Jockman suggested that birds were showing up in unusual places and whales were beaching themselves due to the Earth's changing magnetic grids. It seemed important to me that I begin to use sacred geometry in my personal space to assist with my electromagnetic realignment.

Jockman also said that every ancient Master Mason knew that shape equaled energy. They believed space for "an angel in every angle" was created in the design of their sacred architecture. In keeping with practicing material and non-material realities, I choose to create sacred space in my Earthly realm, as well as in my imagination.

The Altar

In creating my personal space, I begin with an altar, which is the symbol of the integration between the self and the Universe. The altar becomes the center point of balanced energies.

Think of the word *altar* as a noun and *alter* as a verb; what you create and place on your altar will alter your life. Create your altar with intention. Where in your home will you put your altar? What will you place on your altar? Why do you create the altar? Be aware of the power of shape, symbols and intention.

On my altar I have pictures and statues of my spiritual helpers (Christ, Mary, and Buddha) along with a healthy green plant to honor the Earth and to symbolize my prayers for the Earth; I have an angel to represent my gratitude for my unseen helpers; I have a candle that symbolizes both fire and a pathway between Heaven and Earth; I have symbols of my family and friends; I have a rock that was a gift from my father; I have a prayer bowl into which I put the names of family, friends, clients, and situations for special prayer.

If you want a change in your life, alter your altar — with intention and see what happens in your life!

Healing Option

What would you want to have on your altar to alter your life, to increase or enhance your desires?

Would you create this altar in your imaginal world or in your physical world?

Sacred Space

Sometimes I am able to create a sacred circle on Earth in which to offer prayers, but most often I create the sacred space in my imagination. Jockman suggested that from the center point within the circle you, with your intentions, become a participant in the creation of your world. At this point, in the center of the sacred circle, all worlds of existence diverge and converge. The single point represents the zero dimension. This center point is the beginning of all shapes of sacred geometry. Expand a point in space and you create a geometric form.

In my imagination I create the center point where I place myself. From there, I expand the space into a circle which surrounds me. I imagine the energy stretching in all directions until it creates a perfect circular sphere. I then imagine a dot directly above my head. I enhance the energy in the circle by imagining it moving in a clockwise circle as the energy from the Universe enters the space at the point above my head. The energy builds within as it moves.

In my mind, I place four equidistant dots on the circle, creating a base square within the circle. I then connect that space with the dot over my head. I now have a pyramid within the circular sphere. Again, I enhance the energy within this space. Here I can energize myself with the energy of the Universe. I also create this space for my counseling office or around my home, to offer up prayers for myself and for others.

As with all of life's activities, intention is crucial; it is even more important in the ritual of creating sacred space where the energy is greatly increased. Intention and sacred space will enhance the manifestations of your prayers and of your living affirmations. It also will increase the speed in which things are manifested. Sacred space is powerful!

HEALING PLACES

There are healing places in our physical world — beautiful mountains, the beach, our home, churches, hospitals, or the embrace of a loved one, but healing places can also be created in the non-material, imaginal realm.

The Sun

I sit in meditation. My intention is to energize my body.

A few deep breaths and I am moving at the speed of light towards a huge ball of Light.

Suddenly, I am speeding toward the Sun so fast I cannot figure out how to stop! I'll be burned to a crisp.

Zap into the Center. Surprise, I didn't burn up. In fact, it does not even feel hot. What is this place?

I am taken to what looks like an ice or crystal pyramid, just large enough for me to kneel within on a meditation stool. As I sit within, Gentle Beings move around the pyramid, as if adjusting the energy focused on me.

I seem to be in some type of rejuvenation place. It feels great. Here in the middle of the sun, I just soak in the rays.

When it is time to leave, I am instantly home, stretching like a kitten waking up from a nap in the sun. I feel better.

This is a place I visit often whenever I am a little low on energy.

Healing Option

Sit quietly. Breathe deeply. Let your mind drift. What instant vacation can you create in your mind for your own rejuvenation?

The Healing Chamber

My knees and back hurt; I feel a cold coming on. I call upon my guide, Asumi, to see if he will accompany me to the healing chamber.

It looks like stainless steel but it is soft, like clouds. Maybe it is the diffused Light that makes it look so soft. It is warm and womb-like and comfortable. I like this place.

I am on a table that seems to rotate up, down and around, as appropriate, suspended in the air. The table also looks like stainless steel, but it is also warm and comfortable. It feels as if I am floating above the table a few inches.

There are Beings adjusting some instruments and I find myself in a warm flow of Light. I am asked about specific needs. I indicate my knees, my back, and the cold. Laser type lights are directed at my body. I bask in the healing of the warm lights and the laser lights.

I am not sure where I am when I ask for this healing place, where others are attending to me. Maybe this is my spiritual hospital.

Are these real places? Ah, yes, the *real* question. Well, I use my healing places for a lot of my emotional and physical aches and pains. If thought creates, then using imagination to re-create seems logical.

One of my premises for life:

If it works, keep doing it.

If it does not work, do something else!

My healing places work to increase the Light within me. What can you create to assist you in your healing, to increase your clarity and vibration as a Light Worker.

Putting It All Together

I do not know if I will experience Ascension in my lifetime. What I have discovered, though, in my search for peace, is that as I clear up old business and more quickly learn my lessons, I experience more peace and joy. I handle the chaotic times more easily. I truly believe that I am making more space inside me for Light. I am more compassionate than ever before. My body has fewer aches and pains than when I was 20 years old. Things just do not bother me as much as they used to. I feel better as I get older!

I no longer have a fear of death. I will welcome it. Meanwhile, I will practice being in the NOW and being aware of my thoughts as I co-create my reality on Earth. I will follow my commitment to do the work of Spirit on Earth, until I no longer have use on Earth. I am a Light Worker. I walk with intention. I take action. I come to Earth with purpose.

During the period of my mother's youth, there were no self-help books, no workshops, and no therapists. How fortunate we are to have such assistance with our miracles. I encourage you to undertake your own journey for there is now a plethora of useful information for your healing. Most of all, I encourage you to nurture your own wise self, for the one who knows

ALL is you! Your greatest teacher lies within.

I believe we live in the best of times. It may even get more wonderful! In my own life, I am surrounded by people who love and support me. I am in good health. I love what I do. I was blessed with a wonderful extended family. Even with everything that has happened in my life and in spite of the "stuff" I still have to face in this chaotic, changing world, I am grateful to be on Earth at this time. I will continue to work in multitudes of realities in the material and non-material worlds to facilitate my healing and the healing of others.

Today is a beautiful autumn day. It is also my late mother's birthday. I think I will visit her in Heaven and wish her Happy Birthday!

I settle into my chair, take a few deep breaths and set my intention for Mom.

I meet her in some swirling clouds. She has chosen a lively, youthful presence for her time in this space. She looks lovely — and happy. I tell her I have come to wish her Happy Birthday. She hugs me in delight and says *Come. I have something to show you.*

I follow her to a door in the clouds. Opening it I see wondrous Light. I turn to Mom, but she says *No, this trip is my birthday gift to you.* I am deeply moved by her love. Tears come to my eyes as I move through the door of *her* birthday gift to me.

I am just floating around in this wonderful space — in this brilliant Light — just being nurtured and supported.

I hear a voice: *What do you want? You can have, or be, anything you want.*

The question catches me off guard. I think for a moment, and then say I want to be taller and thinner. And so it is. So this is how thought creates. This is great!

What else do you want?

Awkwardly, I realize I do not really know what I want. It is a very strange feeling to experience this instant creation — moment by moment. I play with creation for a time, all the while thinking I probably should give some more concrete thought to what I really want.

As the time of my instant creation gift draws to a close, I exit the door to my waiting mother. What a ride!

She says, *Come. We are celebrating.* Sure enough, there is the whole family of relatives gathered for her Earth birthday. Many of these people I have not seen for years and years. It is a great party.

As I get ready to leave for my reality on Earth, Mom says, *Look, I have one more gift to show you.*

I turn to look at my Earth home. I am in awe. All around the planet are open doors with this wondrous Light shining through onto Earth. I am seeing all the doorways of Heaven opened up with Light freely flowing to the Earth. It is magnificent. I am blessed to be living on an Earth with so much Heavenly Light!

I hug Mom and then I am home, knowing the gates of Heaven are open. Something really big has happened on Earth. I am so grateful. The doors of the veil have opened. Now is the time for Heaven on Earth!

To all of you who have journeyed with me in this book, live in peace and joy, on Earth as it is in Heaven,

BIBLIOGRAPHY

Bach, Richard. *Illusions: The Adventures of a Reluctant Messiah*. New York: Dell Publishing Co., Inc., 1979.

Beck, Renee, and Sydney Barbara Metrick. *The Art of Ritual: A Guide to Creating and Performing Your Own Rituals for Growth and Change*. Berkeley: Celestial Arts, 1990.

Braden, Gregg. *Awakening to Zero Point: The Collective Initiation*. 3rd ed. Bellevue, WA: Radio Bookstore Press, 1997.

Braden, Gregg. *Walking Between the Worlds: The Science of Compassion*. Bellevue, WA: Radio Bookstore Press, 1997.

Brooke Medicine Eagle. "Awakening in the Golden Age." Audiocassette. Sebastopol, CA: Harmony Network, 1996.

Carroll, Lee. *Don't Think Like a Human! Kryon Book II*. Del Mar: The Kryon Writings, 1996.

Carroll, Lee. *Alchemy of The Human Spirit: A Guide to Human Transition into the New Age, Kryon Book III.* Del Mar: The Kryon Writings, 1996.

Fickes, Bob. *Ascension: The Time Has Come . . .* Mount Shasta: Council of Light, Inc., 1991.

Foos-Graber, Anya. *Deathing: An Intelligent Alternative for the Final Moments of Life.* York Beach, ME: Nicholas-Hays, Inc., 1989.

Hendricks, Gay and Kathlyn Hendricks. *Radiance! Breathwork, Movement and Body-Centered Psychotherapy.* Berkeley: Wingbow Books, 1991.

Hendricks, Gay and Kathlyn Hendricks. *At the Speed of Life: A New Approach to Personal Changes Through Body-Centered Therapy.* Bantam Books: New York, 1993.

Jochmans, Joseph Robert. "Journeys into Meta-Creation." Chron. 2. Blaine, WA: Alma Tara Publishing, 1997.

Joy, W. Brugh. *Joy's Way: A Map for the Transformational Journey.* Los Angeles: J.P. Tarcher, Inc., 1979.

Kalweit, Holger. *Dreamtime and Inner Space: The World of the Shaman.* Boston: Shambhala, 1988.

Karpinski, Gloria D. *Where Two Worlds Touch: Spiritual Rites of Passage.* New York: Ballantine Books, 1990.

Klein, Eric. *The Crystal Stair: A Guide to the Ascension.* 2nd ed. Livermore, CA: Oughten House Publications, 1992.

Krippner, Stanley, ed. *Dreamtime and Dreamwork: Decoding the Language of the Night.* Los Angeles: J.P. Tarcher, Inc., 1990.

Monroe, Robert A. *Journeys Out of the Body.* New York: Doubleday, 1977.

Monroe, Robert A. *Far Journeys.* New York: Doubleday, 1985.

Monroe, Robert A. *Ultimate Journey.* New York: Doubleday, 1994.

Moody, Raymond A. *Reflections on Life After Life.* New York: Bantam Books, Inc., 1977.

Mookerjee, Ajit. *Kundalini: The Arousal of the Inner Energy.* 3rd ed. Rochester, VT: Destiny Books, 1986.

Redfield, James. *The Celestine Prophecy: An Adventure.* New York: Warner Books, Inc., 1993.

Redfield, James and Carol Adrienne. *The Tenth Insight: Holding the Vision.* New York: Warner Books, 1996.

Silva, Jose and Philip Miele. *The Silva Mind Control Method.* New York: Pocket Books, 1977.

Small, Jacquelyn. *Transformers: The Therapists of the Future.* Marina del Rey: De Vorss and Co., 1982.

Sogyal Rinpoche. *The Tibetan Book of Living and Dying.* New York: HarperCollins Publishers, 1993.

Sogyal Rinpoche. "Tonglen: The Practice of Giving and Receiving." *Tricycle: The Buddhist Review*, 7, no.1, Fall 1997.

Stone, Joshua David. *The Easy-to-read Encyclopedia of the Spiritual Path: The Complete Ascension Manual.* Sedona: Light Technology Publishing, 1994.

Stone, Joshua David. *Hidden Mysteries: ETs, Ancient Mystery Schools and Ascension.* Sedona: Light Technology Publishing, 1995.

Tachi-ren, Tashira. *What is Lightbody?* 2nd ed. Livermore, CA: Oughten House Publications, 1990.

Tunneshende, Merilyn. *Medicine Dream.* Charlottesville: Hampton Roads Publishing Co., Inc., 1996.

Did you borrow this book?

Want a copy of your own?

Need a great gift for a friend or loved one?

Yes, I want to invest $9.95 in my future and have a personal copy of this book. Send me _____ copies of *Living in Chaos, Walking in Peace: A Matter of Ascension.*

Please add $2.00 per book for postage and handling. Idaho residents include 5% state sales tax in the amount of $.50 per book. Send check payable to :

Legendary Publishing Company
Lorry Roberts, Publisher
P.O. Box 7706
Boise, Idaho 83707-1706

Print Name _____

Address _____

City _____ State _____ Zip _____

Living in Chaos, Walking in Peace $9.95 x ___ # books = _____

Postage and Handling $2.00 x ___ # books = _____

Idaho Tax $ .50 x ___ # books = _____

Enclosed is my check/money order
                    for the total amount of $ _____

Quantity Orders Invited
For bulk discount prices, please call:
(208) 342-7929
Please photo copy this page if additional forms are needed.